I0473185

Hearing Conservation

U.S. Department of Labor
Elaine L. Chao, Secretary

Occupational Safety and Health Administration
John L. Henshaw, Assistant Secretary

OSHA 3074
2002 (Revised)

Contents

Hearing Conservation

OSHA Assistance, Services, and Programs

OSHA Regional and
Area Office Directory

OSHA-Approved
Safety and Health Plans

OSHA Consultation Projects

Hearing Conservation

What is occupational noise exposure?

Noise, or unwanted sound, is one of the most pervasive occupational health problems. It is a by-product of many industrial processes. Sound consists of pressure changes in a medium (usually air), caused by vibration or turbulence. These pressure changes produce waves emanating away from the turbulent or vibrating source. Exposure to high levels of noise causes hearing loss and may cause other harmful health effects as well. The extent of damage depends primarily on the intensity of the noise and the duration of the exposure.

Noise-induced hearing loss can be temporary or permanent. Temporary hearing loss results from short-term exposures to noise, with normal hearing returning after period of rest. Generally, prolonged exposure to high noise levels over a period of time gradually causes permanent damage.

OSHA's hearing conservation program is designed to protect workers with significant occupational noise exposures from hearing impairment even if they are subject to such noise exposures over their entire working lifetimes.

This publication summarizes the required component of OSHA's hearing conservation program for general industry. It covers monitoring, audiometric testing, hearing protectors, training, and recordkeeping requirements.

What monitoring is required?

The hearing conservation program requires employers to monitor noise exposure levels in a way that accurately identifies employees exposed to noise at or above 85 decibels (dB) averaged over 8 working hours, or an 8-hour time-weighted average (TWA). Employers must monitor all employees whose noise exposure is equivalent to or greater than a noise exposure received in 8 hours where the noise level is constantly 85 dB. The exposure measurement must include all continuous, intermittent, and impulsive noise within an 80 dB to 130 dB range and must be taken during a typical work situation. This requirement is performance-oriented because it allows employers to choose the monitoring method that best suits each individual situation.

Employers must repeat monitoring whenever changes in production, process, or controls increase noise exposure. These changes may mean that more employees need to be included in the program or that their hearing protectors may no longer provide adequate protection.

Employees are entitled to observe monitoring procedures and must receive notification of the results of exposure monitoring. The method used to notify employees is left to the employer's discretion.

Employers must carefully check or calibrate instruments used for monitoring employee exposures to ensure that the measurements are accurate. Calibration procedures are unique to specific instruments. Employers should follow the manufacturer's instructions to determine when and how extensively to calibrate the instrument.

What is audiometric testing?

Audiometric testing monitors an employee's hearing over time. It also provides an opportunity for employers to educate employees about their hearing and the need to protect it.

The employer must establish and maintain an audiometric testing program. The important elements of the program include baseline audiograms, annual audiograms, training, and followup procedures. Employers must make audiometric testing available at no cost to all employees who are exposed to an action level of 85 dB or above, measured as an 8-hour TWA.

The audiometric testing program followup should indicate whether the employer's hearing conservation program is preventing hearing loss. A licensed or certified audiologist, otolaryngologist, or other physician must be responsible for the program. Both professionals and trained technicians may conduct audiometric testing. The professional in charge of the program does not have to be present when a qualified technician conducts tests. The professional's responsibilities include overseeing the program and the work of the technicians, reviewing problem audiograms, and determining whether referral is necessary.

The employee needs a referral for further testing when test results are questionable or when related medical problems are suspected. If additional testing is necessary or if the employer suspects a medical pathology of the ear that is caused or aggravated by wearing hearing protectors, the employer must refer the employee for a clinical audiological evaluation or otological exam, as appropriate. There are two types of audiograms required in the hearing conservation program: baseline and annual audiograms.

What is a baseline audiogram?

The baseline audiogram is the reference audiogram against which future audiograms are compared. Employers must provide baseline audiograms within 6 months of an employee's first exposure at or above an 8-hour TWA of 85 dB. An exception is allowed when the employer uses a mobile test van for audiograms. In these instances, baseline audiograms must be completed within 1 year after an employee's first exposure to workplace noise at or above a TWA of 85 dB. Employees, however, must be fitted with, issued, and required to wear hearing protectors whenever they are exposed to noise levels above a TWA of 85 dB for any period exceeding 6 months after their first exposure until the baseline audiogram is conducted.

Baseline audiograms taken before the hearing conservation program took effect in 1983 are acceptable if the professional supervisor determines that the audiogram is valid. Employees should not be exposed to workplace noise for 14 hours before the baseline test or wear hearing protectors during this time period.

What are annual audiograms?

Employers must provide annual audiograms within 1 year of the baseline. It is important to test workers' hearing annually to identify deterioration in their hearing ability as early as possible. This enables employers to initiate protective followup measures before hearing loss progresses. Employers must compare annual audiograms to baseline audiograms to determine whether the audiogram is valid and whether the employee has lost hearing ability or experienced a standard threshold shift (STS). An STS is an average shift in either ear of 10 dB or more at 2,000, 3,000, and 4,000 hertz.

What is an employer required to do following an audiogram evaluation?

The employer must fit or refit any employee showing an STS with adequate hearing protectors, show the employee how to use them, and require the employee to wear them. Employers must notify employees within 21 days after the determination that their audiometric test results show an STS. Some employees with an STS may need further testing if the professional determines that their test results are questionable or if they have an ear problem thought to be caused or aggravated by wearing hearing protectors. If the suspected medical problem is not thought to be related to wearing hearing protection, the employer must advise the employee to see a physician. If subsequent audiometric tests show that the STS identified on a previous audiogram is not persistent, employees whose exposure to noise is less than a TWA of 90 dB may stop wearing hearing protectors.

The employer may substitute an annual audiogram for the original baseline audiogram if the professional supervising the audiometric program determines that the employee's STS is persistent. The employer must retain the original baseline audiogram, however, for the length of the employee's employment. This substitution will ensure that the same shift is not repeatedly identified. The professional also may decide to revise the baseline audiogram if the employee's hearing improves. This will ensure that the baseline reflects actual hearing thresholds to the extent possible. Employers must conduct audiometric tests in a room meeting specific background levels and with calibrated audiometers that meet American National Standard Institute (ANSI) specifications of SC-1969.

When is an employer required to provide hearing protectors?

Employers must provide hearing protectors to all workers exposed to 8-hour TWA noise levels of 85 dB or above. This requirement ensures that employees have access to protectors before they experience any hearing loss.

Employees must wear hearing protectors:

- For any period exceeding 6 months from the time they are first exposed to 8-hour TWA noise levels of 85 dB or above, until they receive their baseline audiograms if these tests are delayed due to mobile test van scheduling;

- If they have incurred standard threshold shifts that demonstrate they are susceptible to noise; and

- If they are exposed to noise over the permissible exposure limit of 90 dB over an 8-hour TWA.

Employers must provide employees with a selection of at least one variety of hearing plug and one variety of hearing muff. Employees should decide, with the help of a person trained to fit hearing protectors, which size and type protector is most suitable for the working environment. The protector selected should be comfortable to wear and offer sufficient protection to prevent hearing loss.

Hearing protectors must adequately reduce the noise level for each employee's work environment. Most employers use the Noise Reduction Rating (NRR) that represents the protector's ability to reduce noise under ideal laboratory conditions. The employer then adjusts the NRR to reflect noise reduction in the actual working environment.

The employer must reevaluate the suitability of the employee's hearing protector whenever a change in working conditions may make it inadequate. If workplace noise levels increase, employees must give employees more effective protectors. The protector must reduce employee exposures to at least 90 dB and to 85 dB when an STS already has occurred in the worker's hearing. Employers must show employees how to use and care for their protectors and supervise them on the job to ensure that they continue to wear them correctly.

What training is required?

Employee training is very important. Workers who understand the reasons for the hearing conservation programs and the need to protect their hearing will be more motivated to wear their protectors and take audiometric tests. Employers must train employees exposed to TWAs of 85 dB and above at least annually in the effects of noise; the purpose, advantages, and disadvantages of various types of hearing protectors; the selection, fit, and care of protectors; and the purpose and procedures of audiometric testing. The training program may be structured in any format, with different portions conducted by different individuals and at different times, as long as the required topics are covered.

What exposure and testing records must employers keep?

Employers must keep noise exposure measurement records for 2 years and maintain records of audiometric test results for the duration of the affected employee's employment. Audiometric test records must include the employee's name and job classification, date, examiner's name, date of the last acoustic or exhaustive calibration, measurements of the background sound pressure levels in audiometric test rooms, and the employee's most recent noise exposure measurement.

Beginning January 1, 2003, employers also will be required to record work-related hearing loss cases when an employee's hearing test shows a marked decrease in overall hearing. Employers will be able to make adjustments for hearing loss caused by aging, seek the advice of a physician or licensed health-care professional to determine if the loss is work-related, and perform additional hearing tests to verify the persistence of the hearing loss.

OSHA Assistance, Services, and Programs

How can OSHA help me?

OSHA can provide extensive help through a variety of programs, including assistance about safety and health programs, state plans, workplace consultations, voluntary protection programs, strategic partnerships, alliances, and training and education. An overall commitment to workplace safety and health can add value to your business, to your workplace, and to your life.

How does safety and health management system assistance help employers and employees?

Working in a safe and healthful environment can stimulate innovation and creativity and result in increased performance and higher productivity. The key to a safe and healthful work environment is a comprehensive safety and health management system.

OSHA has electronic compliance assistance tools, or eTools, on its website that "walk" users through the steps required to develop a comprehensive safety and health program. The eTools are posted at www.osha.gov, and are based on guidelines that identify four general elements critical to a successful safety and health management system:

- Management leadership and employee involvement,

- Worksite analysis,

- Hazard prevention and control, and

- Safety and health training.

What are state programs?

The *Occupational Safety and Health Act of 1970 (OSH Act)* encourages states to develop and operate their own job safety and health plans. OSHA approves and monitors these plans and funds up to 50 percent of each program's operating costs. State plans must provide standards and enforcement programs, as well as voluntary compliance activities, that are at least as effective as Federal OSHA's.

Currently, 26 states and territories have their own plans. Twenty-three cover both private and public (state and local government) employees and three states, Connecticut, New Jersey, and New York, cover only the public sector. For more information on state plans, see the list at the end of this publication, or visit OSHA's website at www.osha.gov.

What is consultation assistance?

Consultation assistance is available on request to employers who want help establishing and maintaining a safe and healthful workplace. Funded largely by OSHA, the service is provided at no cost to small employers and is delivered by state authorities through professional safety and health consultants.

What is the Safety and Health Achievement Recognition Program (SHARP)?

Under the consultation program, certain exemplary employers may request participation in OSHA's Safety and Health Achievement Recognition Program (SHARP). Eligibility for participation includes, but is not limited to, receiving a full-service, comprehensive consultation visit, correcting all identified hazards, and developing an effective safety and health program management program.

Employers accepted into SHARP may receive an exemption from programmed inspections (not complaint or accident investigation inspections) for 1 year initially, or 2 years upon renewal. For more information about consultation assistance, see the list of consultation projects at the end of this publication.

What are the Voluntary Protection Programs (VPPs)?

Voluntary Protection Programs are designed to recognize outstanding achievements by companies that have developed and implemented effective safety and health management programs. There are three levels of VPPs: Star, Merit, and Demonstration. All are designed to achieve the following goals:

- Recognize employers that have successfully developed and implemented effective and comprehensive safety and health management programs;

- Encourage these employers to continuously improve their safety and health management programs;

- Motivate other employers to achieve excellent safety and health results in the same outstanding way; and

- Establish a cooperative relationship between employers, employees, and OSHA.

VPP participation can bring many benefits to employers and employees, including fewer worker fatalities, injuries, and illnesses; lost-workday case rates generally 50 percent below industry averages; and lower workers' compensation and other injury- and illness-related costs. In addition, many VPP sites report improved employee motivation to work safely, leading to a better quality of life at work; positive community recognition and interaction; further improvement and revitalization of already-good safety and health programs; and a positive relationship with OSHA.

After a site applies for the program, OSHA reviews an employer's VPP application and conducts a VPP onsite evaluation to verify that the site's safety and health management programs are operating effectively. OSHA conducts onsite evaluations on a regular basis, annually for participants at the demonstration level, every 18 months for Merit, and every 3 to 5 years for Star. Once a year, all participants must send a copy of their most recent annual internal evaluation to their OSHA regional office. This evaluation must include the worksite's record of injuries and illnesses for the past year.

Sites participating in VPP are not scheduled for regular, programmed inspections. OSHA does, however, handle any employee complaints, serious accidents, or significant chemical releases that may occur at VPP sites according to routine enforcement procedures.

Additional information on VPP is available from OSHA national, regional, and area offices listed at the end of this booklet. Also, see "Cooperative Programs" on OSHA's website.

How can a partnership with OSHA improve worker safety and health?

OSHA has learned firsthand that voluntary, cooperative partnerships with employers, employees, and unions can be a useful alternative to traditional enforcement and an effective way to reduce worker deaths, injuries, and illnesses. This is especially true when a partnership leads to the development and implementation of a comprehensive workplace safety and health management program.

What is OSHA's Strategic Partnership Program (OSPP)?

OSHA Strategic Partnerships are agreements among labor, management, and government to improve workplace safety and health. These partnerships encourage, assist, and recognize the efforts of the partners to eliminate serious workplace hazards and achieve a high level of worker safety and health. Whereas OSHA's Consultation Program and VPP entail one-on-one relationships between OSHA and individual worksites, most strategic partnerships build cooperative relationships with groups of employers and employees.

There are two major types of OSPPs. Comprehensive partnerships focus on establishing comprehensive safety and health management systems at partnering worksites. Limited partnerships help identify and eliminate hazards associated with worker deaths, injuries, and illnesses, or have goals other than establishing comprehensive worksite safety and health programs.

For more information about this program, contact your nearest OSHA office or visit the agency's website.

What occupational safety and health training does OSHA offer?

The OSHA Training Institute in Arlington Heights, IL, provides basic and advanced training and education in safety and health for federal and state compliance officers, state consultants, other federal agency personnel, and private-sector employers, employees, and their representatives.

What is the OSHA Training Grant Program?

OSHA awards grants to nonprofit organizations to provide safety and health training and education to employers and workers in the workplace. Grants often focus on high-risk activities or hazards or may help nonprofit organizations in training, education, and outreach.

OSHA expects each grantee to develop a program that addresses a safety and health topic named by OSHA, recruit workers and employers for the training, and conduct the training. Grantees are also expected to follow up with students to find out how they applied the training in their workplaces.

For more information contact OSHA Office of Training and Education, 2020 Arlington Heights Road, Arlington Heights, IL 60005; or call (847) 297–4810.

What other assistance materials does OSHA have available?

OSHA has a variety of materials and tools on its website at www.osha.gov. These include eTools such as Expert Advisors and Electronic Compliance Assistance Tools, information on specific health and safety topics, regulations, directives, publications, videos, and other information for employers and employees.

OSHA also has an extensive publications program. For a list of free or sales items, visit OSHA's website at www.osha.gov or contact the OSHA Publications Office, U.S. Department of Labor, 200 Constitution Avenue, NW, N-3101, Washington, DC 20210. Telephone (202) 693–1888 or fax to (202) 693–2498.

In addition, OSHA's CD-ROM includes standards, interpretations, directives, and more. It is available for sale from the U.S. Government Printing Office. To order, write to the Superintendent of Documents, U.S. Government Printing Office, Washington, DC 20402, or phone (202) 512–1800.

What do I do in case of an emergency or to file a complaint?

To report an emergency, file a complaint, or seek OSHA advice, assistance, or products, call (800) 321–OSHA or contact your nearest OSHA regional, area, state plan, or consultation office listed at the end of this publication. The teletypewriter (TTY) number is (877) 889–5627.

Employees can also file a complaint online and get more information on OSHA federal and state programs by visiting OSHA's website at www.osha.gov.

OSHA Regional and Area Office Directory

OSHA Regional Offices

Region I

(CT,* MA, ME, NH, RI, VT*)
JFK Federal Building, Room E340
Boston, MA 02203
(617) 565–9860

Region II

(NJ,* NY,* PR,* VI*)
201 Varick Street, Room 670
New York, NY 10014
(212) 337–2378

Region III

(DE, DC, MD,* PA,* VA,* WV)
The Curtis Center
170 S. Independence Mall West
Suite 740 West
Philadelphia, PA 19106-3309
(215) 861–4900

Region IV

(AL, FL, GA, KY,* MS,
NC,* SC,* TN*)
SNAF
61 Forsyth Street SW, Room 6T50
Atlanta, GA 30303
(404) 562–2300

Region V

(IL, IN,* MI,* MN,* OH, WI)
230 South Dearborn Street,
Room 3244
Chicago, IL 60604
(312) 353–2220

Region VI

(AR, LA, NM,* OK, TX)
525 Griffin Street, Room 602
Dallas, TX 75202
214) 767–4731 or 4736 x224

Region VII

(IA,* KS, MO, NE)
City Center Square
1100 Main Street, Suite 800
Kansas City, MO 64105
(816) 426–5861

Region VIII

(CO, MT, ND, SD, UT,* WY*)
1999 Broadway, Suite 1690
PO Box 46550
Denver, CO 80202-5716
(303) 844–1600

Region IX

(American Samoa, AZ,*
CA,* HI, NV,* Northern
Mariana Islands)
71 Stevenson Street, Room 420
San Francisco, CA 94105
(415) 975–4310

Region X

(AK,* ID, OR,* WA*)
1111 Third Avenue, Suite 715
Seattle, WA 98101-3212
(206) 553–5930

---

*These states and territories operate their own OSHA-approved job safety and health programs. The Connecticut, New Jersey, and New York plans cover public employees only. States with approved programs must have a standard that is identical to, or at least as effective as, the federal standard.

OSHA Area Offices

Anchorage, AK
(907) 271–5152

Birmingham, AL
(205) 731–1534

Mobile, AL
(251) 441–6131

Little Rock, AR
(501) 324–6291/5818

Phoenix, AZ
(602) 640–2348

Sacramento, CA
(916) 566–7471

San Diego, CA
(415) 975–4310

Denver, CO
(303) 844–5285

Greenwood Village, CO
(303) 843–4500

Bridgeport, CT
(203) 579–5581

Hartford, CT
(860) 240–3152

Wilmington, DE
(302) 573–6518

Fort Lauderdale, FL
(954) 424–0242

Jacksonville, FL
(904) 232–2895

Tampa, FL
(813) 626–1177

Savannah, GA
(912) 652–4393

Smyrna, GA
(770) 984–8700

Tucker, GA
(770) 493–6644/6742/8419

Des Moines, IA
(515) 284–4794

Boise, ID
(208) 321–2960

Calumet City, IL
(708) 891–3800

Des Plaines, IL
(847) 803–4800

Fairview Heights, IL
(618) 632–8612

North Aurora, IL
(630) 896–8700

Peoria, IL
(309) 671–7033

Indianapolis, IN
(317) 226–7290

Wichita, KS
(316) 269–6644

Frankfort, KY
(502) 227–7024

Baton Rouge, LA
(225) 389–0474/0431)

Braintree, MA
(617) 565–6924

Methuen, MA
(617) 565–8110

Springfield, MA
(413) 785–0123

Linthicum, MD
(410) 865–2055/2056

Bangor, ME
(207) 941–8177

Portland, ME
(207) 780–3178

Lansing, MI
(517) 327–0904

Minneapolis, MN
(612) 664–5460

Kansas City, MO
(816) 483–9531

St. Louis, MO
(314) 425–4249

Jackson, MS
(601) 965–4606

Billings, MT
(406) 247–7494

Raleigh, NC
(919) 856–4770

Bismark, ND
(701) 250–4521

Omaha, NE
(402) 221–3182

Concord, NH
(603) 225–1629

Avenel, NJ
(732) 750–3270

Hasbrouck Heights, NJ
(201) 288–1700

Marlton, NJ
(856) 757–5181

Parsippany, NJ
(973) 263–1003

Carson City, NV
(775) 885–6963

Albany, NY
(518) 464–4338

Bayside, NY
(718) 279–9060

Bowmansville, NY
(716) 684–3891

New York, NY
(212) 337–2636

North Syracuse, NY
(315) 451–0808

Tarrytown, NY
(914) 524–7510

Westbury, NY
(516) 334–3344

Cincinnati, OH
(513) 841–4132

Cleveland, OH
(216) 522–3818

Columbus, OH
(614) 469–5582

Toledo, OH
(419) 259–7542

Oklahoma City, OK
(405) 278–9560

Portland, OR
(503) 326–2251

Allentown, PA
(610) 776–0592

Erie, PA
(814) 833–5758

Harrisburg, PA
(717) 782–3902

Philadelphia, PA
(215) 597–4955

Pittsburgh, PA
(412) 395–4903

Wilkes–Barre, PA
(570) 826–6538

Guaynabo, PR
(787) 277–1560

Providence, RI
(401) 528–4669

Columbia, SC
(803) 765–5904

Nashville, TN
(615) 781–5423

Austin, TX
(512) 916–5783/5788

Corpus Christi, TX
(361) 888–3420

Dallas, TX
(214) 320–2400/2558

El Paso, TX
(915) 534–6251

Fort Worth, TX
(817) 428–2470
(817) 485–7647

Houston, TX
(281) 591–2438/2787

Houston, TX
(281) 286–0583/0584/5922

Lubbock, TX
(806) 472–7681/7685

Salt Lake City, UT
(801) 530–6901

Norfolk, VA
(757) 441–3820

Bellevue, WA
(206) 553–7520

Appleton, WI
(920) 734–4521

Eau Claire, WI
(715) 832–9019

Madison, WI
(608) 264–5388

Milwaukee, WI
(414) 297–3315

Charleston, WV
(304) 347–5937

OSHA-Approved Safety and Health Plans

Alaska Department of Labor and Workforce Development

Commissioner
(907) 465–2700
FAX: (907) 465–2784

Program Director
(907) 269–4904
FAX: (907) 269–4915

Industrial Commission of Arizona

Director, ICA
(602) 542–4411
FAX: (602) 542–1614

Program Director
(602) 542–5795
FAX: (602) 542–1614

California Department of Industrial Relations

Director
(415) 703–5050
FAX: (415) 703–5114

Chief
(415) 703–5100
FAX: (415) 703–5114

Manager, Cal/OSHA
Program Office
(415) 703–5177
FAX: (415) 703–5114

Connecticut Department of Labor

Commissioner
(860) 566–5123
FAX: (860) 566–1520

Conn–OSHA Director
(860) 566–4550
FAX: (860) 566–6916

Hawaii Department of Labor and Industrial Relations

Director
(808) 586–8844
FAX: (808) 586–9099

Administrator
(808) 586–9116
FAX: (808) 586–9104

Indiana Department of Labor

Commissioner
(317) 232–2378
FAX: (317) 233–3790

Deputy Commissioner
(317) 232–3325
FAX: (317) 233–3790

Iowa Division of Labor

Commissioner
(515) 281–6432
FAX: (515) 281–4698

Administrator
(515) 281–3469
FAX: (515) 281–7995

Kentucky Labor Cabinet

Secretary
(502) 564–3070
FAX: (502) 564–5387

Federal/State Coordinator
(502) 564–3070, x240
FAX: (502) 564–1682

Maryland Division of Labor and Industry

Commissioner
(410) 767–2999
FAX: (410) 767–2300

Deputy Commissioner
(410) 767–2992
FAX: 767–2003

Assistant Commissioner, MOSH
(410) 767–2215
FAX: 767–2003

Michigan Department of Consumer and Industry Services

Director
(517) 322–1814
FAX: (517) 322–1775

Minnesota Department of Labor and Industry

Commissioner
(651) 296–2342
FAX: (651) 282–5405

Assistant Commissioner
(651) 296–6529
FAX: (651) 282–5293

Administrative Director,
OSHA Management Team
(651) 282–5772
FAX: (651) 297–2527

Nevada Division of Industrial Relations

Administrator
(775) 687–3032
FAX: (775) 687–6305

Chief Administrative Officer
(702) 486–9044
FAX: (702) 990–0358

[Las Vegas (702) 687–5240]

New Jersey Department of Labor

Commissioner
(609) 292–2975
FAX: (609) 633–9271

Assistant Commissioner
(609) 292–2313
FAX: (609) 292–1314

Program Director, PEOSH
(609) 292–3923
FAX: (609) 292–4409

New Mexico Environment Department

Secretary
(505) 827–2850
FAX: (505) 827–2836

Chief
(505) 827–4230
FAX: (505) 827–4422

New York Department of Labor

Acting Commissioner
(518) 457–2741
FAX: (518) 457–6908

Division Director
(518) 457–3518
FAX: (518) 457–6908

North Carolina Department of Labor

Commissioner (919) 807–2900
FAX: (919) 807–2855

Deputy Commissioner,
OSH Director
(919) 807–2861
FAX: (919) 807–2855

OSH Assistant Director
(919) 807–2863
FAX: (919) 807–2856

Oregon Occupational Safety and Health Division

Administrator
(503) 378–3272
FAX: (503) 947–7461

Deputy Administrator for Policy
(503) 378–3272
FAX: (503) 947–7461

Deputy Administrator for Operations
(503) 378–3272
FAX: (503) 947–7461

Puerto Rico Department of Labor and Human Resources

Secretary
(787) 754–2119
FAX: (787) 753–9550

Assistant Secretary for Occupational Safety and Health
(787) 756–1100/1106, 754–2171
FAX: (787) 767–6051

Deputy Director for Occupational Safety and Health
(787) 756–1100, 1106/754–2188
FAX: (787) 767–6051

South Carolina Department of Labor, Licensing, and Regulation

Director
(803) 896–4300
FAX: (803) 896–4393

Program Director
(803) 734–9644
FAX: (803) 734–9772

Tennessee Department of Labor

Commissioner
(615) 741–2582
FAX: (615) 741–5078

Acting Program Director
(615) 741–2793
FAX: (615) 741–3325

Utah Labor Commission

Commissioner
(801) 530–6901
FAX: (801) 530–7906

Administrator
(801) 530–6898
FAX: (801) 530–6390

Vermont Department of Labor and Industry

Commissioner
(802) 828–2288
FAX: (802) 828–2748

Project Manager
(802) 828–2765
FAX: (802) 828–2195

Virgin Islands Department of Labor

Acting Commissioner
(340) 773–1990
FAX: (340) 773–1858

Program Director
(340) 772–1315
FAX: (340) 772–4323

Virginia Department of Labor and Industry

Commissioner
(804) 786–2377
FAX: (804) 371–6524

Director, Office of Legal Support
(804) 786–9873
FAX: (804) 786–8418

Washington Department of Labor and Industries

Director
(360) 902–4200
FAX: (360) 902–4202

Assistant Director
[PO Box 44600]
(360) 902–5495
FAX: (360) 902–5529

Program Manager,
Federal–State Operations
(360) 902–5430
FAX: (360) 902–5529

Wyoming Department of Employment

Safety Administrator
(307) 777–7786
FAX: (307) 777–3646

OSHA Consultation Projects

Anchorage, AK
(907) 269–4957

Tuscaloosa, AL
(205) 348–3033

Little Rock, AR
(501) 682–4522

Phoenix, AZ
(602) 542–1695

Sacramento, CA
(916) 263–2856

Fort Collins, CO
(970) 491–6151

Wethersfield, CT
(860) 566–4550

Washington, DC
(202) 541–3727

Wilmington, DE
(302) 761–8219

Tampa, FL
(813) 974–9962

Atlanta, GA
(404) 894–2643

Tiyam, GU
9–1–(671) 475–1101

Honolulu, HI
(808) 586–9100

Des Moines, IA
(515) 281–7629

Boise, ID
(208) 426–3283

Chicago, IL
(312) 814–2337

Indianapolis, IN
(317) 232–2688

Topeka, KS
(785) 296–2251

Frankfort, KY
(502) 564–6895

Baton Rouge, LA
(225) 342–9601

West Newton, MA
(617) 727–3982

Laurel, MD
(410) 880–4970

Augusta, ME
(207) 624–6400

Lansing, MI
(517) 322–1809

Saint Paul, MN
(651) 284–5060

Jefferson City, MO
(573) 751–3403

Pearl, MS
(601) 939–2047

Helena, MT
(406) 444–6418

Raleigh, NC
(919) 807–2905

Bismarck, ND
(701) 328–5188

Lincoln, NE
(402) 471–4717

Concord, NH
(603) 271–2024

Trenton, NJ
(609) 292–3923

Santa Fe, NM
(505) 827–4230

Albany, NY
(518) 457–2238

Henderson, NV
(702) 486–9140

Columbus, OH
(614) 644–2631

Oklahoma City, OK
(405) 528–1500

Salem, OR
(503) 378–3272

Indiana, PA
(724) 357–2396

Hato Rey, PR
(787) 754–2171

Providence, RI
(401) 222–2438

Columbia, SC
(803) 734–9614

Brookings, SD
(605) 688–4101

Nashville, TN
(615) 741–7036

Austin, TX
(512) 804–4640

Salt Lake City, UT
(801) 530–6901

Montpelier, VT
(802) 828–2765

Richmond, VA
(804) 786–6359

Christiansted St. Croix, VI
(809) 772–1315

Olympia, WA
(360) 902–5638

Madison, WI
(608) 266–9383

Waukesha, WI
(262) 523–3044

Charleston, WV
(304) 558–7890

Cheyenne, WY
(307) 777–7786

www.ingramcontent.com/pod-product-compliance
Lightning Source LLC
Chambersburg PA
CBHW071601170526
45166CB00004B/1747